Anger Management
12 Simple Ways to Control Your Emotions, Develop Self-Control, and Minimize Your Day-to-Day Stress

Table of Contents

Introduction

Before we get started, I would like to thank and congratulate you for downloading your copy of *Anger Management: 12 Simple Ways to Control Your Emotions, Develop Self-Control, and Minimize Your Day-to-Day Stress*. By reading this brief but information-packed guide, you are taking the first steps towards gaining control over your anger and freeing yourself from your intense emotions.

If you're one of the countless people who struggle with anger, you've no doubt seen the havoc that uncontrollable rage wreaks on your relationships, career, and well-being. Even if you're not the explosive type, being constantly grumpy and quickly irritated takes a toll on your mind and body. Others become uneasy around you, and you don't even feel comfortable in your own skin. No doubt you feel frustrated with others, but you could be feeling frustrated with yourself, too.

If this sounds familiar, it's time to start asking yourself some difficult questions. Where is all this anger coming from? How much of it is really justified? Is your life truly as difficult as you think, or are you letting your anger make it harder than it needs to be? How do you draw the line between expressing your anger in a healthy way and just taking it out on others?

The answers to these questions will not come easily, but with some digging, you can start to find the wisdom that you need to regain control and ease your relationships with others. Life with extreme anger is challenging, and getting through each day can seem like navigating an obstacle course of intense emotions—but it doesn't have to stay that way.

The good news is: if you're reading this now, you've decided to take control and guide yourself in a healthier direction. Change is possible, and you do have what it takes to stay calm and carry on. With dedicated effort and a lot of self-honesty, you can and will develop the self-control that you need to bring harmony and peace to your life.

As you read through this book, you'll find ways to answer your questions about your anger in addition to learning essential skills for coping with and overcoming your anger. I have a lot to share with you, and I hope you are as eager as I am to get this process underway. Without further ado, let's begin.

Chapter 1: Accept Your Anger

One of the reasons that anger is perhaps the most difficult emotion to cope with is the stigma that society places around the expression of anger. In some ways, it is more acceptable to display grief and fear than it is to display anger. People often seem to have this perception that anger makes a person less "good" or "virtuous" in character.

Of course, this simply is not true. If it were, we would not have a single person in the world we could consider good or virtuous, because everyone gets angry eventually. However, despite the misconception, the damage is done when it comes to shutting down an open dialogue. The stigma surrounding anger means that we don't raise our children with knowledge of how to process and cope with anger in healthy ways—which means that we weren't taught how to deal with anger, either.

When we aren't given the tools to properly cope with our anger, we use whatever ways our instincts first bring to mind. Unfortunately, instinct is not the best judge when it comes to decision-making. Letting instinct decide how we react to a situation that makes us angry means that we usually choose courses of action that hurt others and ourselves. To remedy this, we must first give ourselves permission to accept what is happening and then resolve to correct the problem.

Accepting a part of ourselves that society has deemed to be dangerous or undesirable can be difficult and uncomfortable. However, accepting our anger is the first crucial step to learning to overcome the hold it has over us. As countless gurus and self-help experts have attested, acceptance is the key to liberation.

Anger is Natural

As evolutionary psychologists have pointed out, anger is as natural as any other human instinct. We feel anger when we feel threatened in some way as an evolutionary instinct to protect our resources and families. As soon as we start to feel threatened, our brain triggers the release of adrenaline and cortisol to prompt a swift response so that we have a better chance of successfully shutting down the threat. Biologically speaking, those who were quickest to respond—quickest to anger—were more likely to scare away or kill a predator or aggressor, making it more likely that their genes would carry on into the next generation.

However, times have changed quite a lot and far fewer of us live in conditions that make quick tempers and hyper-aggression necessary responses to perceived threats. More often it is our egos, rather than our lives, that are on the line when we feel threatened by others and uncontrollable situations.

That being said, anger is a completely natural human emotion that almost everyone experiences. In fact, never feeling anger might be just as unhealthy as experiencing excessive anger. A healthy level of anger means that we have a sense of right and wrong, that we know when we are being treated unfairly, and that we are willing to stand up for ourselves when we experience injustice. When channeled in a healthy and productive way, anger can help us to overcome barriers to our success and well-being.

So, next time you start to feel the anger sharks swimming around in your head, rather than feel ashamed of what's happening, know that your anger is completely natural.

Some—But Not All—of Your Anger is Probably Justified

When we first realize that our anger is excessive and out of control, our tendency might be to swing the pendulum in the far opposite direction and tell ourselves that we have no reason to be angry. However, invalidating our emotions can be just as destructive as overindulging them. Coping with anger in a healthy way means finding a balance between your thoughts and emotions and the reality of the situation at hand—and balance means avoiding "all or nothing" types of thinking.

It is here that we first begin to ask ourselves those critical questions about the nature of our anger. Is your anger truly justified, or are you overreacting and taking things too personally? Do people truly deserve to be hit with your worst, or are you unfairly taking your anger out on others?

Remember that part of acceptance means allowing yourself to admit that you're not always right. It's okay to make mistakes; we are all human, after all. However, it is not okay to keep treating people badly once you have realized that you are doing so.

To be fair, much of your anger is probably justified. Perhaps you are being treated unfairly by a boss or coworker, or maybe your partner or children are constantly taking advantage of your good will. When these situations of unfairness arise, it is natural and even healthy to feel angry. After all, you can't just stay in an unhealthy situation without standing up for yourself. In these cases, your anger is a good sign that you know how you do and do not deserve to be treated, and hopefully that you're willing to stand up for yourself when necessary.

It is in carefully choosing how you respond to a situation that has made you angry that you start to ensure you're not overstepping justifiable anger and unfairly hurting someone else. Just because someone has hurt you first does not mean that you have the right to hurt them back. Part of making mature and healthy decisions means that you learn to forgive others and treat others fairly, even when you are not receiving that same treatment yourself. In the long run, you will gain more respect and be a more effective problem solver when you use your anger to prompt you to act, but then only take those actions that are well thought out and healthy for everyone in the situation.

By accepting your anger as natural and sometimes justifiable, you begin to normalize your feelings and move towards recognizing that you can control how you respond to difficult situations. When you give yourself permission to accept and explore your feelings, you open the door to radical self-honesty and give yourself the ability to recognize when your responses are unfair and hurtful to others. Stop using your anger to threaten and intimidate others into submission, and you'll find that a lot of tension and conflict drain out of your life with that change alone.

Chapter 2: Understand Your Anger

Now that you've learned to accept anger as a natural human emotion, it's time to dig deeper to understand your anger. Why are you experiencing so much anger? How can you stop your temper from exploding before it begins?

Understanding your anger can provide valuable insights into how and why you experience the emotions that you do. From this understanding, you can pick up clues about the best way to address your deeper emotional issues and the environmental factors that contribute to your anger patterns.

Explore the Roots of Your Anger

To every emotion, there is a deeper core embedded in memories from our early experiences. When it comes to anger, those roots can come from many places. While some people formed their anger habits based on early childhood experiences of others' anger, others use anger to mask deeper emotions of hurt, sadness, insecurity, or embarrassment.

For example, our early experiences might have taught us to dissociate from our anger, causing us to suppress it until it comes out in a huge explosion or in smaller, more subtle ways. Perhaps our parents disciplined us severely for throwing temper tantrums, rather than giving us tools to cope with or express our feelings in a healthier way. We don't feel safe displaying anger, so we either wait until we're so angry that we can no longer contain it or we take it out passive aggressively on others, jeopardizing our relationships.

On the other hand, if we grew up in an environment where our caretakers or role models regularly exhibited explosive anger, or if our families yelled and screamed at one another a lot, we might have learned that fighting and getting angry is the appropriate response to perceived threats.

Some of us feel angry more often than others. We use our anger to mask other hurt feelings and we hold our anger in a sort of defiance against what others might think. It's easier to deal with anger and to be aggressive than it is to cope with feelings of insecurity, sadness, vulnerability, and humiliation. Getting angry makes us feel powerful and in control, but in truth, we are not in control when we give in to uncontrollable anger.

Next time you feel a rage coming on, pause for a moment and ask yourself, "What am I really feeling? Am I truly angry at this person/situation, or am I upset about something else?" These insights will teach you a lot about yourself so that you can begin to heal at deeper levels than ever before.

Recognize the Warning Signs

Experts in the field of anger management point out that before we begin to recognize our rising anger, our body gives away what's happening with telltale physical signs of distress. Remember, anger is the body's instinctive response to a threat, so when your body starts to go into a state of heightened tension, it's time to slow down and pay attention to what's going on.

When we first start to become angry, we experience several symptoms: quickened heart rate, tension in our muscles (especially the shoulders), clenching of our hands and jaws, flushed or clammy faces, a feeling of growing hot, tunnel vision or "seeing red," breathing faster and harder, feeling a knot in the stomach, headaches, restlessness, or difficulty concentrating.

As soon as these symptoms start to appear in your body, that's a good indicator that it's time for a quick timeout. One way of recognizing these signs is to practice mindfulness, a practice based in Eastern spiritual tradition that can be applied without subscribing to any particular ideology. Mindfulness is the practice of carefully "watching" your thoughts, emotions, and physical sensations without judging them or responding with further emotions. When you take a moment to step back from the situation and make some objective, detached observations about what's going on inside of you, you'll be stopping your anger dead in its tracks while also gaining some insight about yourself.

Identify Triggers

Once you've observed yourself for a while and gotten some information about your emotional patterns, you can start to piece those patterns together to identify people, places, and situations that trigger your anger. Sometimes anger can become a habit, and we might find ourselves automatically responding to certain situations with anger before anything has actually gone wrong. For example, we might get stressed as soon as we sit in our vehicles if we routinely deal with bad traffic jams on our usual commute, even if the roads are relatively clear and traffic is flowing smoothly.

A certain place or person might be a trigger for your anger if there are painful memories associated with them. If this is the case, you'll definitely want to spend more time working through those past traumas—preferably with a trained expert, such as a therapist or life coach.

When you identify people, places, and situations that regularly trigger your anger, you empower yourself to take steps ahead of time to circumvent your anger. For example, if you know that interacting with a certain coworker tends to grind your gears, you can prepare ahead of time by planning the interaction, visualizing a peaceful and mutually beneficial outcome, and practicing relaxation techniques before the encounter. If possible, you can find ways to avoid putting yourself in situations that arouse your anger, especially if you take the time to find solutions and possible workarounds.

By digging deeper to understand the roots of your emotions, learning to recognize the warning signs, and identifying your usual triggers, you can do a lot to curb your anger and get it under control. Knowledge is power, and if you equip yourself well, you can achieve your emotional goals and greatly improve your well-being.

Chapter 3: Pause Before You React

Your anger has just been triggered. Maybe your kids have ignored your requests to clean their rooms one too many times, or your partner has just said something very insensitive. Perhaps your boss is treating you unfairly, or you've just been handed a traffic ticket that you know you didn't deserve.

The warning signs are all there. Your face feels warm, your breath is coming in quick, shallow bursts, you can feel your pulse up in your temples. Part of you wants to just scream and let the offender have it. Before you do, however, there's a moment there where you're still in control. You haven't exploded yet. You can still choose how to respond to this situation without letting your anger get the better of you.

This is the moment you need to learn to recognize and seize to truly get your anger under control.

Anger Makes Us Dumber

Have you ever noticed how difficult it can be to think of a clever comeback when you're in the middle of a heated argument? Maybe you went home still mulling over the encounter, only to later think up four or five things you wish you had said or done differently. For anyone who's ever lashed out in anger, of course, there is always the bitter regret at the feelings we've hurt with sharp words spoken in anger. "Why did I say that?" you might have later asked yourself. "What was I thinking?"

The answer is that you probably weren't thinking—not really. When we get angry, we engage the sympathetic parts of our brain, or those that are related to heightened emotions and the physical responses they trigger. The effect of this is that as we engage our sympathetic system, it shuts down the parasympathetic system—the part of our brain associated with our ability to reason. The result is that when we're angry, we activate our animal instincts and shut down our human rationality—in other words, we shut down the parts of our brains that make us smart and turn on the parts that make us stupid.

So, if you've ever wondered why you said or did something so dumb in a moment of temper, the fact is that, in that moment, you really were dumber.

Let Logic Take the Wheel

When we get angry, our bodies automatically trigger what's known as "fight or flight" mode. In this state, we either respond with fear and run away from the situation, or we get angry and stand our ground to fight. Our bodies have evolved to protect ourselves from predators, so when you're in a situation with someone or something that feels threatening, your instincts are driving you to "kill" the threat. Thankfully fewer of us translate this instinctual drive to actually try and kill others, but we compensate by trying to "kill" them with words and actions. This is why we might throw out an insult that goes below the proverbial belt for our opponent: the insult is so harsh that it stops them in their tracks, effectively "killing" them.

If we pause to reflect for a moment, however, we'll find very few situations that anger us call for us to respond so harshly. For instance, yelling at a teenage grocery store cashier because our coupon expired is never warranted. Not only is it not the cashier's fault that we made a mistake, but the difference is only a few dollars at most and we often can't do anything to change store policy. The result of our overreaction is that we've angered or frightened the people around us, probably traumatized the cashier (and possibly his manager), and compromised our own wellbeing–all for a couple of dollars.

Pausing for reflection before you overreact in an unpleasant situation gives you time to engage your rationality and hopefully realize that whatever's happening is not worth ruining your day and that of others. Taking a few deep breaths will relax your sympathetic system and give your parasympathetic system time to catch up and regain control so that you don't make the dumb mistake of ruining relationships and hurting yourself and others.

Use Relaxation Techniques to Calm Down

If you find yourself in a situation where you need to calm down quickly, you're in luck. Psychologists and other experts have a repertoire of methods and techniques that you can use to hold your horses and restore your sense of calm.

Possibly the most popular and most effective technique is to simply take a few deep breaths. Breathe in from your diaphragm to expand your whole torso. Hold your breath for a few seconds when your lungs are full, then slowly exhale. After you've done this a few times, your heart rate will begin to slow and the side effects of an adrenaline boost will slowly begin to dissipate. That could give you just enough time to consider the situation carefully and choose a rational response.

Some people find counting slowly in their heads gives them something else to focus on for long enough to calm the immediate flare of anger. Others prefer to repeat a certain word or phrase, such as, "Relax," or "Take it easy." Counting and repeating mantras slows the whirlwind of angry thoughts swirling in your mind, giving you the breakthrough that you might need to observe the situation more objectively.

Another favorite relaxation technique is visualization. If you feel yourself growing tense, angry, or stressed, you can close your eyes and visualize a relaxing scene, such as a warm beach, or recall a pleasant memory. These few moments of visualization will take you out of the immediate situation and help guide you to a place where you're calmer and more collected—and perhaps even happier.

By taking a few moments to calm yourself and think logically when you're starting to feel angry, you can prevent many bad situations from getting worse. Pausing and reflecting long enough to release some of your anger can help you keep things in perspective and give you a chance to find solutions to the issue at hand. When you respond to your anger smarter, you not only keep from making things worse—you might actually find that you're making them better.

Chapter 4: Express Your Anger Calmly

Many people make the mistake of thinking that the best solution for dealing with anger is to make it disappear entirely. The reason this line of thinking is flawed is because they seem to think that "anger management" means no longer feeling anger. The truth is that everyone feels angry—yes, even Buddhist monks; just ask the Dalai Lama—and that anger management means just that: you *manage* your anger, not force it to disappear.

Of course, one of the goals of anger management is to experience anger less frequently, but never getting angry again is not a realistic goal. You're setting yourself up for failure if you think anyone is capable of completely eradicating this very natural and basic human emotion from his or her being.

The other big part of anger management is learning to work through the issues that are truly at the heart of the anger problem. This means communicating with others when you are angry, whether you are mad at them or in a situation where anger unrelated to them will still affect your interactions with them. Clear and honest communication will turn opponents into allies in your efforts to get your anger under control.

Be Assertive About Expressing Your Feelings

Expressing our feelings is never easy. Many of us would rather suppress our anger than open up to others about our emotions. However, trying to suppress anger will only make it worse for us. On the one hand, suppressed anger puts a strain on our bodies that will inevitably lead to illness (especially heart-related diseases) later in life.

On the other hand, strong emotions always find their way out. While we may be able to stop ourselves from exploding, if we haven't completely worked through the anger we're feeling, it'll come out in fits of passive-aggressive behavior, which can do damage to our relationships just as much as an explosive temper can.

The tricky part about expressing your feelings is that you must be assertive about beginning these conversations. If your anger has alienated you from the people in your life, you can't wait for them to approach you about your issues. For those who have been suppressing anger for some time, it's important to stand up for yourself and not just passively endure situations that are hurting you.

The key to effectively expressing your anger is to be assertive but non-confrontational. There's a world of difference between being assertive and being aggressive. When you express your anger assertively, you're taking the initiative to communicate your needs with others and to stand up for yourself. When you're being aggressive, however, you're being pushy and competitive and becoming a threat to others. Wait until you're calm and have thought things through before deciding to open the door of communication about your anger.

Be Direct About Your Needs and Be Specific

People aren't mind-readers. It's important to keep this in mind for a couple of reasons. First, you can't make assumptions about other people's motivations. It might seem like some people are intentionally trying to hurt you, but that isn't always the case. When dealing with anger, the tendency is to project your defensiveness onto everyone else, and you can make mistakes in judgment when your thinking is clouded by anger.

The other reason to keep this in mind is that you can't expect others to read your mind when you're angry. How many of the people you think are "out to get you" are completely oblivious to the effect that their actions are having on you? How many people who know you're angry with them really have no idea why?

If you want to work through your anger and improve your relationships, you need to be direct about your needs and specific about the things that are bothering you. Don't force people to pass tests that they don't know they're taking. Giving someone the silent treatment will only deepen the divide in your relationships and cause more hurt.

If your partner is doing something that drives you crazy, tell them what it is, and be specific. Instead of saying, "You never help around the house," try saying, "I have been washing the dishes every night this week without any help." Follow this up with being direct about your needs, such as, "I've been working nine-hour shifts every day lately and I really need some help with the housework." Ideally, your partner will apologize for being oblivious to the imbalance and agree to help more. If they respond with accusations of their own, it may be time to take a closer look at the relationship itself.

Don't Be Accusatory or Hurtful

As we've seen earlier, anger is your body's way of trying to eliminate a threat, which is what provokes us to "go for the throat" of someone we perceive as threatening. Taking an aggressive or confrontational approach to communication will escalate a situation and cause more problems rather than defusing them.

Relationship experts recommend that you communicate with others by using "I" statements instead of making remarks about the other person. If your coworker is upsetting you by slacking off and pulling down team performance, instead of saying, "You're not pulling your weight around here," try saying, "I feel really upset and discouraged when the team doesn't do well."

Another important part of effective communication is to avoid exaggerating or being melodramatic about the reality of the situation. Don't say to your kids, "You guys NEVER clean your rooms," which you know is unlikely to be true. Similarly, don't say to your partner, "I ALWAYS pay all the bills around here." Not only is such language demoralizing to the other people involved in your conversation, but it also sends a message to you that your anger is 100% justified and that you have the right to tear into others without attempting to filter yourself. Allowing yourself to feel self-righteous will prevent you from taking an honest closer look at yourself and the situation, which impedes your ability to grow beyond your emotional habits.

Always make sure that you're completely calm when initiating a difficult conversation. Starting the conversation in an angry state will only ensure that your anger colors what the other person says, preventing you from listening to them and absorbing their perspective. Communication goes both ways; if you want to be heard, remember to listen as well.

Communication is a skill that must be developed with hard work and dedication. No one is born with perfect communication skills, and if we weren't taught effective communication in early childhood development, that means we must figure much of it out on our own.

Don't worry if your communication doesn't automatically improve overnight. Taking the time to practice these skills will improve them over the course of time, and you'll see far better results than if you never tried at all.

Be patient with yourself and others, and you'll find that communicating your anger calmly will ultimately prove beneficial.

Chapter 5: Practice Empathy

Empathy is a powerful tool for overcoming anger. When we feel anger, we're usually so caught up in our own experience that we forget we're dealing with another living, feeling human being. That human being might be acting like a total jerk at the moment, but that doesn't mean we should forget about their feelings. As our parents and teachers used to tell us, two wrongs don't make a right. Though our anger may be justified, that doesn't give us free reign to fly off the handle.

Empathy is the ability to sense and even feel what others are feeling, and to relate to their experiences as though we are experiencing them ourselves. Anger isolates us in our bodies and traps us in our own heads. When we allow ourselves to empathize with others, however, we end our isolation and open our awareness to other people, which can help a lot with letting go of our anger.

Avoid Making Assumptions

We've said it before and we'll say it again: you and the person you're angry with are not mind readers.

Sometimes people are intentionally mean, but more often when someone hurts us, they don't know that they're doing so. Angry people tend to be the way that they are because they feel the need to constantly defend themselves from perceived threats. Being on constant high alert for threats tends to warp one's thinking, and you can find yourself seeing things that aren't really there. A kind smile can appear as a smirk to someone who has let herself grow paranoid with defensiveness. A casual remark about an issue that means a lot to you can seem like an intentional dig if you're in an angry place.

Before you set all engines to go, though, take a moment to calm down and better assess the situation. What evidence do you really have to support your theory that you're being slighted intentionally? Are you making assumptions about someone else's motives? Are you assuming that they know certain actions will upset you? If you've found that you are making some assumptions and letting them color your perception of a situation, it's a good time to take a step back and perhaps give people the benefit of the doubt until they have reason to prove you otherwise.

You Don't Know What Others Might Be Going Through

A big part of not making assumptions includes admitting that you don't know what others are going through. It's easy enough to get mad and yell obscenities at the person cutting you off in traffic, but what if they're rushing an injured person to the hospital? You can get mad at your coworker for being somewhat short when you say, "Good morning," but maybe he just found out that his mother has been diagnosed with cancer. Your friend who said something insensitive might be coping with an abusive relationship and feeling unable to reach out to anyone for help.

The point is, you never know what someone else is feeling or experiencing. Exploding on someone who is going through a hard time over a minor offense could be pushing them even farther into their negative experience. Of course, not everyone who is rude or insensitive or careless is experiencing a major tragedy, but that doesn't mean that you shouldn't still consider the possibility. Ultimately, you'll always feel better if you err on the side of caution. It's easy to address a recurring issue with someone who is treating you badly, but you can't take back hurtful words or actions that turn out to be undeserved.

Give the Same Compassion You'd Wish to Receive

Perhaps you're not a mind reader, but you can gain a lot of insight through empathizing with others. Empathy comes from closely observing others and understanding the nature of universal human emotions. Your self-exploration will help you a lot with understanding what others are going through.

When you've taken the time to deeply understand the roots of your anger and the feelings underlying them, you'll start to recognize those emotions in others. Your boss who often speaks to you condescendingly is probably masking some deep insecurities of her own. The guy who scoffs at you as you walk by has probably been the subject of bullying himself.

As for you, well, coping with anger isn't exactly easy, is it? Maybe you get mad when you find out at the checkout that your coupon is expired because you're embarrassed. Perhaps you've been embarrassed lots of other times before, and that left you feeling powerless. Anger makes you feel less powerless, so you choose to feel that instead of reliving the pain of the past. Yet deep down, you're hurting inside. Wouldn't you want others to respond to your anger with compassion and understanding, rather than yelling and fighting with you? What if someone said, "It's okay, we all make mistakes. You don't have to feel bad." Would that help you feel understood and less threatened?

Once you gain some understanding of what others might be going through, you can begin to extend to them the same compassion that you would hope to receive. This doesn't mean that you go from being a bull to being a doormat, but you can at least resolve to treat others with respect, if not kindness.

An important thing to keep in mind is that you shouldn't allow yourself to get attached to seeing the results of your compassion. Many people who are hurting could also be misperceiving your intentions based on their own past experiences. Furthermore, those who haven't received much compassion in their lives might not know it when they finally do receive it. It'll take time before they understand the gift you're giving them, and that's okay. Even if they don't perceive or appreciate your care, at least you will, and you'll feel all the better for it.

Compassion and empathy are the gifts that keep on giving. In fact, studies have shown that there are physical health benefits to practicing kindness to others. While sustained anger and stress are hard on your heart, for example, practicing kindness improves your heart health. So, even if you don't see the immediate results of your empathy, in the long run, you're doing good by you when you extend compassion and understanding to others.

Chapter 6: Redirect Your Focus

One of the reasons our anger can get so bad is that we tend to mull things over rather than allowing ourselves to move on. Anger management experts say that when our anger explodes, the incident never comes on suddenly. Rather, our anger has built upon itself over time to gain momentum and build into the explosion that we eventually see. Before then, we have suppressed smaller irritations, holding onto them but never processing and releasing them. Anger stacks upon anger until we reach the critical point and unleash the tiger, so to speak.

This process begins when we hold onto anger, allowing ourselves to replay the moment and wallow in it, rather than working through the experience in a productive manner. The ultimate goal of processing anger, as we will explore in more depth later, is to release the emotion, which keeps us tied to the unpleasant experience. One of the best ways to step out of the moment of our anger is to redirect focus away from the incident and towards something that better serves our wellbeing.

Avoid Ranting

A lot of people tend to rant or vent about something that has angered them. However, while verbally acknowledging that something has occurred to upset you is healthy, going on a long rant or repeatedly ranting about the same topic is quite the opposite. Psychologists say that ranting becomes counterproductive when we continue to relive the moment with each revisiting of it. By revisiting the situation, our anger builds rather than dissipating, which is the supposed purpose of ranting to begin with.

Furthermore, the more we rant about our anger to others, the more we find ourselves believing that our anger is fully justified. Perhaps it is, but on the occasions when it's not, gaining support from others for our perspective hardens us against seeing other perspectives. This means that even when we're right, we work ourselves into a corner where we are absolutely right and the other person is absolutely wrong so that we stop trying to understand their position.

Over time, staying in the mindset of self-righteousness, as we've said earlier, can be detrimental to your ability to dig deeper with yourself and others. If you really want to manage your anger and be a better person, avoid giving yourself blind spots by allowing yourself to get into a self-righteous frame of mind.

Find Something Productive to Think About

Too often when we get caught in a mind loop about something that triggered our anger, we waste that mental energy that we could be spending on something more productive. Anger has a tendency to hijack our focus, making it difficult to concentrate as we obsess over what we said, what the other person said, and what we could have done differently.

In the time that you spend reflecting on the subject of your anger, your anger grows and spreads its roots in your psyche. That's time that could be spent constructively trying to find a solution to the issues, or focusing on matters that are far more important to you. Think of it this way: every minute you spend angry is a minute that you're taking away from your life.

Do you have an interest that you're truly passionate about? Do you wish you could spend more quality time with your family and friends? Do you have a secret dream that you wish to accomplish, such as building a business or traveling more?

Every minute that you spend on anger is a minute you could be spending on accomplishing your goals. If you come home angry from work and fester in your bad mood rather than enjoying the company of your kids, there's an opportunity for quality time lost. If you call up a friend just so that you can rant about your boss, that's time you could be spending on research for your new business, or working on a hobby that you're passionate about.

So, how do you stop the cycle of wasting time on anger? Take a few moments to write down your top three goals. These could be related to your career, hobbies, lifestyle dreams, or your relationships. Try to choose only those goals that make you feel happy, inspired, motivated, and optimistic. Goals that make you feel guilty or stressed (i.e., "Oh, I should really be drawing up that business plan. How can I be taking so long on this task?") are generally best avoided for this exercise.

Once you have your goals written down, get into the habit of carrying your list around with you, in your wallet or pocket, and reading it over regularly. Then, next time you start obsessing over a situation that has made you angry, take a few deep breaths and read over your list again. Gently guide your focus away from the source of your anger and towards dreaming about your goals. If you can, it might be helpful to draw up a quick to-do list of next steps for yourself. Otherwise, just focus on enjoying the outcomes of achieving your goals and let the pleasure motivate you to move on in a more productive direction.

It's Okay to Distract Yourself

Sometimes when we're angry, we're also tired. When we get like this, we don't want to focus on goals, or trying harder, or doing much of anything, really. When moments like these pop up, know that it's okay to distract yourself with things that require less energy on your part.

If you're a social media enthusiast, you might make the conscious decision to scroll through some newsfeeds for a few minutes until your mood picks up. Or perhaps you have some articles saved that you've been meaning to read, or a book that you're enjoying, or some videos or movies that you love to watch. If you're really having a hard time shaking a bad mood, it's okay to simply distract yourself with things that might cheer you up.

On a precautionary note, if you're worried that distractions might take over your attention and prevent you from doing things that matter to you (i.e., you really want to spend time in the garden, but you keep getting sucked into Facebook and lose daylight), you might want to put a cap on how much time you can spend on these distractions. Give yourself a time limit—20 minutes, an hour, whatever works for you —and then when time is up, turn your focus back to more productive matters.

Set Reminders for Yourself

If you're having a hard time remembering to redirect your focus to more productive things, try setting some reminders for yourself. You can set alarms on your phone for every couple of hours that remind you to read over your list of goals. You can post sticky notes around your home or office with little reminders about your goals.

Placing pictures or items that make you feel relaxed and happy where you can see them often can also serve as a helpful reminder to focus on the positive and let go of the negative. Get creative with finding ways to knock yourself out of a bad mood and get back on track.

Just as with anything else, getting into the habit of redirecting your focus to something more productive will take time to build. Don't get frustrated with yourself if it takes a while for you to learn to do this more regularly. Brooding over an issue that has upset you occasionally, isn't the end of the world. Only you can know whether you feel you're benefitting more from obsessing over a bad situation or focusing on something that makes you happy.

Chapter 7: Channel Your Anger Creatively

Creative expression is a human drive so universal that even our cavemen ancestors were doing it. Something in the human spirit needs to be expressed in ways that go beyond the everyday mundane communication. Creative expression has helped us to explore those deeper parts of ourselves and the world around us for countless millennia, and it seems to come as naturally to us as breathing.

Psychologists can't stop raving about the psychological benefits of using creative hobbies to process, communicate, and release intense emotions. Creative pursuits put us into a meditative frame of mind, giving us something to focus on so that we feel safe to explore those aspects of ourselves that we might otherwise avoid.

Channeling your anger creatively can not only help you to relax, but you might also reach a deeper understanding of yourself and the people around you.

Find a Hobby that Relaxes and Interests You

Whether you choose painting, dancing, jogging, writing, swimming, crocheting, horseback riding, playing an instrument, or any other type of creative pursuit, it's important to find something that you like to do. Ideally you will also find this hobby relaxing. Hobbies that stress you out or don't interest you won't be very good for helping you channel your anger. Choose something that you like doing and that you find relatively relaxing.

Hobbies are a great way to knock yourself out of an angry mood and redirect your focus to something that brings you pleasure. Even if time is a concern for you, find ways that you can spend even 15 minutes a day working on your hobby. After all, aren't your health and wellbeing worth taking a few minutes out of every day to ensure?

Much of the time our anger arises when we feel trapped in a situation or in our particular set of circumstances. Having a hobby that we enjoy can give us something that takes us outside of our bad situation, transporting us to a place where there are no stresses or cares—just us and our passion. Finding something that you can turn to that helps the whole world to fall away can be one of the best things you ever do for yourself in your efforts to effectively manage your anger.

Express Yourself

Aside from giving you something to focus on and helping you to relax, there are many creative outlets that can help you to express your unique feelings. Hobbies like painting, writing, dancing, drawing, photography, and the like are especially great avenues for communicating your anger.

Sometimes our emotions come from a place inside of us that goes much deeper than the surface reason for our upset. This place is not one that we can understand by merely scratching the surface; we need to dig deeper to find the emotional sources of our feelings and behavioral patterns.

Creative expression can help you to work through your deeper issues by giving you other ways to look at and communicate them. We can't always figure things out just by sitting and thinking them through. Different people process feelings and thoughts differently. If you're a visual person, visual art can help you to put your feelings in a context that you better understand. Similarly, a person who processes information best through auditory learning might find that music is the best outlet for them. Some people are very words oriented, and that could make writing a perfect channel for their creative expression.

The most important thing is that you find an outlet that resonates with you deeply. As long as you feel that your feelings are being expressed, that's the most important part.

Do It for You

We can all get a little self-conscious when it comes time to learn a new skill or share our work with others. If we're just starting out with a new creative pursuit, we tend to think that we're not good enough at our hobby, and perhaps we never will be. "What would others think if they saw our work?" we wonder.

Don't give in to this type of thinking. Especially when you're using creative outlets for therapeutic purposes, all that matters is how you feel. If your painting is relaxing you and making you happy, don't worry about what anyone else would think of your work. If you're really enjoying knitting but all your initial efforts are coming out as though a child were attempting them, resist the temptation to judge yourself. *Everyone* starts somewhere, and no one ever starts out perfect.

The benefits of creative expression are many, but the most important part is that your hobbies make you feel better than you did before. Whether you prefer to pursue relaxing hobbies that help you to forget all your stresses, or you choose to express your emotions creatively to help you process and communicate them, you'll be glad for the efforts you put into learning something new.

Chapter 8: Release Your Anger with Exercise

Exercise is one of the best ways to burn through frustration and help release anger. Anger experts highly recommend that people working through any mental and emotional issues, especially anger, spend at least 30 minutes per day getting some physical exercise. In fact, that's the standard for everyone, so those struggling with anger issues have even more incentive to take expert medical advice and get some much-needed exercise.

Find a Vigorous Activity that You Enjoy

As we saw earlier, anger triggers the nervous system by releasing adrenaline. When we experience an adrenaline rush, our muscles tense for action. Standing still in these circumstances will make us feel tense, anxious, and jittery. Often the best solution for this excess of energy is to burn it off through vigorous exercise.

The best way to release pent-up energy from anger is to find a vigorous physical activity that you enjoy. Whether you prefer running, swimming, hiking, lifting weights, riding a bike, fencing, or any other kind of sport or exercise is entirely up to you. The key is to make sure that your chosen activity helps you release your anger and any excess adrenaline you might have in your system.

Sustained anger is especially hard on our hearts. To counter this, it's best to build heart health with regular cardio exercises. A good rule of thumb is that if it gets your heart rate up and makes you sweat, you're doing it right.

Always be sure to consult with a healthcare professional before undertaking any fitness regimen. If you have preexisting health concerns, take care when starting new exercises and talk to your doctor about how to exercise safely.

Avoid Yelling, Punching, or Other Violent Activities

As tempting as it may be to release anger with more violent activities, such as yelling, punching, or fighting, anger management experts advise against it. Yelling or screaming, even just into a pillow, reinforces the anger rather than helping to defuse it. Not only that, but training your mind that it's okay to scream when you get angry will increase the likelihood that you'll resort to yelling and screaming at others in the heat of the moment.

Similarly, punching, kicking, and fighting, as satisfying as they might be, also increases the likelihood that you'll swing a punch at the next person who ticks you off. If you prefer boxing or martial arts as a sport, that doesn't mean you have to stop engaging in these activities—just don't do them when you're mad. Only undertake full contact sports when you're calm and in a good mood, then find other ways to work through your anger in the moment. If you're angry when you show up to the gym, run or lift it off, and then turn to the punching bag once you feel calmer.

You should also refrain from imagined violence. As tempting as it might be to imagine clocking the guy who cut us in line, if you repeatedly feed your brain these images, you might find yourself doing it unconsciously next time you see red. Not only will you hurt the other person for what is probably a minor offense, but you'll land yourself in a world of trouble for letting your anger get out of control.

Get Good Sleep, and Stay Hydrated

While we're on the subject of physical health, other factors that will help you keep your anger under control include getting a decent amount of sleep every night, eating a well-balanced diet, and staying hydrated. Sleep deprivation, dehydration, and hunger all contribute to higher levels of stress, which will make you more easily irritated and more likely to experience a temper flare up. Don't force yourself to run on empty tanks. Get a full night of sleep every night, drink plenty of water, and avoid skipping meals. Remember that this is your health we're talking about, and taking the time to mind it is worth your effort.

We really can't overemphasize the importance of getting good exercise and leading a healthy lifestyle. Again, these things are all best practice for everyone, and they become even more important for those working through anger management. Make time in your schedule for daily exercise, sleep, and proper nourishment, and see what a difference those changes alone can make.

Chapter 9: Give Yourself a Break

Many people with anger management issues find themselves in situations where they're overworked and overstressed. As the pressure builds, it becomes harder to take a few moments to recharge and recover your balance. Yet when life gets stressful, that's exactly the time that you should be allowing yourself to take a break.

Build Breaks into Your Work Schedule

Productivity experts say that one of the best ways to increase efficiency and productivity at work is to take frequent breaks. The Pomodoro Technique, first developed by Francesco Cirillo, is a popular time management technique that many productivity experts swear by. In this technique, you'd break your work blocks into 25-minute segments, and then take a 5-minute break at the end of that time. After three time blocks, or an hour and a half, you would take a longer 30-minute break to eat a snack, take a short walk, etc.

The concept behind this technique is that the brain naturally works in waves of sustained attention and activity, then experiences a natural crash at the end of 25 minutes and then 90 minutes of sustained activity. By working with these natural neural cycles, rather than trying to push through them, you help your brain to stay charged so that you get more done.

The main point to walk away from with this is that we need breaks to stay healthy and productive. For many of us living in Western societies, we place a lot of emphasis on working hard and staying busy. This has helped foster a belief that needing to take breaks is a sign of weakness, yet the truth is quite the opposite. The best way to boost productivity is to give yourself breaks and avoid burning out. After all, even if you sit at your desk for 10 hours, you're no good if you're dragging and fighting brain fog to try and get things done.

Take a Timeout If You Get Too Stressed

When you feel tension building and you know that you're entering the danger zone for setting off your anger, give yourself permission to take a break and calm down. As stressed as you might be, you'll lose a lot more time over a meltdown than you would from giving yourself a 10-minute break to de-stress.

As we saw in Chapter 6, you can spend your break redirecting your focus to get your mind off of your stress for a few minutes. You can distract yourself with a cute video, looking through pictures of your kids or pets, or browsing the internet for articles about things that inspire and motivate you.

You'll also want to practice some of the relaxation techniques from Chapter 3. Take some deep breaths, repeat a mantra, visualize a peaceful scene, or take a short walk to guide yourself out of the stress zone. By taking the time to release your stress, you'll keep your anger from growing and getting out of control.

Communicate Your Needs to Others

Nobody likes to admit when they're struggling with something. The stigma is all the worse when it comes to mental health. However, if you have a high-stress job that demands a lot of time and energy, or if you live in a chaotic environment, or have a lot of pressure at school, don't be afraid to communicate with your peers, loved ones, and superiors about ways that they can help you succeed.

You'll find that people are very willing to help when they know you are facing a challenge. You can tell your boss, teacher, or human resources manager in confidence that you're working through anger management, and you need to be able to take breaks to calm down when you're feeling stressed. They might even help to relieve your workload to help make things easier on you. Surely, they'd much rather have you come to them for help so you can work through issues together than to unknowingly push you into a crisis.

Your loved ones can also help you when you're having a difficult time making some big changes. Your family can help you to stay calm by agreeing to set quiet times at certain parts of the day, such as for the first 20 minutes after you get home from work. Friends can send you reminder texts to make sure that you're taking breaks throughout your day. If you have little kids, find ways that they can be safely alone for 15 minutes at a time so that you can step away and relax, and ask friends and family to babysit when things become too overwhelming.

Never be ashamed to admit when you need help. You'll find that most people in your life will be all too happy to lend a helping hand.

No matter how high the pressure is on you, you're no good at all if you push yourself to a breaking point. When anger is an issue, the breaking point doesn't just include physical illness and disease as it does for others, but you have the added danger of having an anger meltdown. Take these breaks seriously and you'll find that your health and temper benefit enormously.

Chapter 10: Seek Solutions to Your Issues

Sometimes anger doesn't just come from what's going on inside of us. Sometimes it's our physical circumstances that have us on edge and stressed out. This could be the case when we're in dire financial circumstances, when we're dealing with an illness in ourselves or in the family, when we're stuck at an unfulfilling and demanding job, or when we're in a bad relationship.

As stressful as your situation might be, focusing on the negative aspects of the situation and your anger will only make it worse. Rather than pouring your energy into the emotional black hole of anger, you could be working to find solutions to the issues that are causing you to be so frequently upset.

Perhaps the solutions are not readily apparent. You might be in an especially tricky situation, and maybe it could take a lot of time to make a significant change. However, if you give up on finding solutions and resign yourself to your frustration, things really will never get better, will they? It's far better to take your time searching for solutions and eventually find one than to never try at all.

Change Your Situation

Often, we find ourselves in situations that aren't completely bad, but we'd feel a lot better if some things were different. Perhaps we have a job that we like well enough, but the pay isn't high enough or the workload is too heavy. Or maybe we're in a relationship with someone we really love, but that person has some habits that we find hard to live with.

When you find yourself in a situation that you don't want to leave but you can't handle as is, it's time to look for ways to change things. Take a few minutes to sit down with pen and paper, and draw a line down the center of the page. In one column write things that are good about your situation, then in the other column write things that aren't so good. If you've determined that the good generally outweighs the bad, or that it could if some of the bad things were different, then it's worth your time to try making some changes.

Next, take your list of things that need to change and write about how you would prefer those things to be. If you're not getting enough hours at the job you love, you might write that you would prefer more hours. Be specific. If you know that you need at least 36 hours a week at a job to make ends meet, then write that down.

Finally, start brainstorming ways that you could make some changes to improve your circumstances. If you need more hours at work, a lighter workload, or to not work with a particular team member, try talking to your boss about your needs and see if you can work together toward a solution. If your partner is driving you crazy with particular habits, talk to them calmly and see if you can both make some changes that would improve the relationship.

Be willing to compromise when necessary. Remember that taking small steps toward creating the changes you want could take some time, and be patient. Perhaps your boss can't offer you 40 hours per week now, but he can offer 33 and says you might be able to earn more as you improve your performance and gain rank through seniority. Maybe your partner is willing to make some changes, but they have a hard time remembering to always adapt the new habits you agreed on. Accept what you can get and then work to improve things as you go along.

Get Out of a Bad Situation

Some situations are so bad that it's really not worth our time to try and make them work. Maybe we're working a job where the boss is unwilling to compromise and has abusive management tactics. Perhaps we're in a relationship with a partner who is not open to change and continues to do things we find hurtful or disrespectful no matter how many times we raise the issue.

When we've run up against a wall, it's time to break out of our bad situation. Of course, that's always easier said than done, but it's never impossible. You can look for a new job and leave when you find one. Maybe it's hard to find a job that will immediately satisfy your needs, but you can take another part time job or enroll in classes as a step toward making your way out.

If you're in a bad relationship situation and you can't immediately exit it because you're living with that person and can't afford housing on your own, there are options. You can search Craigslist for people looking for roommates, apply for government housing grants, move in with friends or relatives, and so on.

There are always options if you get creative and commit to searching for them. Be persistent, be patient, and believe in yourself, and you will get through.

Learn to Accept Your Situation

Occasionally, we find ourselves in a situation that, try as we might, we simply can't get out of. These are very rare, but when they do arise, they are extremely frustrating, demoralizing, and sad. If you've found yourself in a situation that you genuinely can't change or leave, then it might be time to start accepting your circumstances.

The key to understanding this lesson comes in the knowledge that, though you may not be able to change your external circumstances, you can always change yourself. For instance, you can change the way you relate to a person or situation by deciding that you're not going to let the problem get to you in the same way. If your boss is continually rude, don't let him get under your skin. Know that his issues are about him and not about you, then let it go. If you're dealing with an illness, be grateful for the fortunes that you do have and make your peace.

Only you can know when it's time to accept your circumstances, and how best to go about that. If adopting a spiritual practice or finding support groups appeal to you, then go for it. Those are great outlets for not only learning how to accept your situation, but for letting go of the negative emotions that come along with it.

No matter what your situation, there is always a solution in some form. As long as you're willing to seek it out, the answer will come to you.

Chapter 11: Lighten Up with Humor

There is no rule against lightening up. You really don't have to be so serious all the time.

Anger management experts suggest that humor can be one of the most effective tools for curbing your anger. Part of the reason is that much of our anger comes from taking ourselves too seriously. When we start slipping into the mentality where we're right and everyone else is wrong, that isn't an accurate depiction of reality to being with. Hence, humor can help us to keep things in perspective.

The other reason that humor can be so helpful with anger management is that laughter counters the tension we release when we start to become angry. After all, it's hard to hold onto a bad mood when you're grinning from ear to ear, isn't it?

Laughter is the Best Medicine

Laughter is one of the best cures for a mounting temper. We often resist the impulse to laugh or smile when we're angry because we want to indulge the building tension, rather than allow it to dissipate prematurely. Our bodies can become addicted to certain neurochemicals over time. For instance, the longer we subject our brains to high amounts of anger, the more active the receptors in our brain that pertain to anger become. Meanwhile, the neurotransmitters that are responsible for regulating the other emotions, such as happiness and peacefulness, start to atrophy from lack of use. In essence, we can literally rewire our brains to favor angry responses to stimulus over other responses.

The good news is that we can counter that pattern by consciously rewiring our brains with humor. Every time you disrupt your anger with humor, you break the cycle of chemical "addiction" and give your brain room to form new habits.

Aside from that, laughter provides additional benefits to the body. Not only does laughing decrease the amount of stress hormones in the body, but it also gives a huge boost to the immune system. Every time you laugh, your body produces more antibodies and immune cells. Not only that, but laughter triggers the release of endorphins, the "feel-good" hormone in the body that relieves pain and promotes a sense of wellbeing.

Use Humor in the Moment

It is best to employ humor in the precise moment that you feel a rage coming on. Once you've gotten into the habit of pausing before you choose to react, you can choose to see the situation at hand with a sense of humor.

For instance, if the barista messes up your beverage in the morning, take a moment to imagine a ludicrous scenario to lighten your mood. "I'm sure this barista has been waiting all morning to take her anger out on someone," you might say. "She's probably been plotting this elaborate revenge for months, just waiting for the right person to come along and exact it on."

By clearly exaggerating the severity of the situation, you can help keep your ego in check and remind yourself that the real situation isn't nearly as dire as you were about to make it out to be in your head.

Don't Be Sarcastic or Cynical

Your first attempts at humor in an angry moment might not be as successful as you would hope. It'll take a while for humor to feel natural. You might find yourself resorting to sarcasm as part of you continues to hold onto your anger.

Difficult as it might be, try to avoid resorting to sarcasm or cynicism. When spoken aloud, your sarcastic or cynical words can hurt others just as much as purely angry words can.

Moreover, sarcasm and cynicism naturally breed bitterness—another self-defense mechanism that will leave you feeling crummy in the long run. If you can't bring yourself to use humor purely, you might decide to just stick with the relaxation techniques, but for those who can make it work, a little bit of humor is a great way to boost one's mood and move on to the next thing.

Chapter 12: Forgive and Let Go

One of the most difficult and yet most fundamental aspects of anger management is learning the art of forgiveness. Much of our anger stems from feeling that we have been deeply wronged in some way by the other person. While this may or may not actually be true, reacting to them with anger will not necessarily see that the wrong gets set right. In many cases, people are reluctant to admit when they have done something wrong, and we may never get the apology that we feel we deserve.

Think of it this way: holding onto anger means that you get hurt twice as much as you otherwise were originally. The first time you get hurt is at the moment that the bad or unfair thing happens. The second time is when you get angry. Anger will ruin your mood and possibly your day if you allow it to. So really, by getting angry, you take that moment and extend it for as long as you hold onto the emotion and the memory.

This is why forgiveness is so essential. By learning to forgive and move on, you ensure that you don't prolong the unpleasant experience with unnecessary suffering and give yourself the ability to move on with your life.

Don't Hold Grudges

A grudge can become very destructive if we allow ourselves to hold onto it. Think about it: what's the longest you've ever held a grudge? There are some people who can hold a grudge for their entire lives, continuing to hate someone who hurt them in grade school well into their middle and later age. When you stop to think about it, the person who hurt them back then is so different from the person who likely exists now that the past individual doesn't even exist anymore. Why hold onto anger towards a person who is essentially dead to the world?

If you're nursing hard feelings toward someone who is no longer in your life, or who has moved on, all you're doing is keeping yourself from moving on. You're trapping yourself in that moment. Let it go and be free.

Learn to Forgive Yourself and Others

The sooner you learn to forgive others, the sooner you will drain your reserve of anger in your life. If someone hurts you or irritates you in the present, forgive them as soon as you can. It'll be one less thing you have to feel bad about.

Similarly, you'll do well by yourself to learn to forgive things you have said or done in the past. As long as you've learned from the mistakes you made and are resolving to be a better person, holding onto anger or guilt from the past only ensures that you're more likely to make further mistakes in the future. Again, let it go and move forward.

Moving Forward

On the note of moving forward, that can be easier said than done. When we've held onto anger for so long, it can be hard to envision a future without anger and resentment. However, you must visualize this future for yourself if you have any hope of creating the possibility of change for yourself.

Change is scary. It doesn't matter who you are; everyone has a moment of fear before making a big change in life. Trust the advice on this one: you'll feel a lot better after facing down your fear than you will if you choose to stay in the place that is making you and those you love so unhappy. You know perfectly well what the status quo holds, so dare to let it go and give yourself the opportunity to create something new and wonderful in your life.

Forgiveness isn't easy, but like every other skill offered in this book, it will come more easily with practice. Practicing empathy is one of the best ways to cultivate compassion towards others, which will give you the boost you need to understand how others in the situation might be feeling. Once you understand others, you'll have a much easier time softening your position, and you'll open the door to releasing anger and creating the sense of peace that you deserve.

Conclusion

Thank you for reading through to the end! I hope you found the advice in this book helpful. With hard work and dedication, you will have what it takes to curb your anger and get your emotions under control.

Beyond this book, you have a myriad of resources available to help you on your quest to build a better life for yourself without excessive anger. There are plenty of anger management therapists and support groups who are ready to give you loving and judgment-free guidance as you progress in your unique healing journey. You can also find online forums, workshops, and webinars dedicated to helping those who struggle with anger management. No matter what, you never must face this challenge alone.

Finally, if you found the information in this book helpful or inspiring, chances are that others will, too! A positive review on Amazon will ensure that others find and access the guidance available in this book, and it will be much appreciated.

Thanks again, and I wish you the best of luck.

Made in the USA
San Bernardino, CA
11 February 2018